The Workers' Detective

The Workers' Detective

A Story about Dr. Alice Hamilton

by Stephanie
Sammartino McPherson

illustrations by Janet Schulz

A Carolrhoda Creative Minds Book

Carolrhoda Books, Inc./Minneapolis

To my husband, Dick, with thanks for his support and encouragement

Special thanks to the Fort Wayne and Allen County Public Libraries, Indiana; Connecticut College Archives; and the Lyme Public Library, Lyme, Connecticut

Library of Congress Cataloging-in-Publication Data

McPherson, Stephanie Sammartino.
     The workers' detective : a story about Dr. Alice Hamilton / by Stephanie Sammartino McPherson ; illustrated by Janet Schulz.
         p.   cm. — (A Creative minds book)
     Includes bibliographical references.
     Summary: A biography of Dr. Alice Hamilton, social worker and doctor, whose work brought attention to the health risks associated with particular jobs.
     ISBN 0-87614-699-X (lib. bdg.)
     1. Hamilton, Alice, 1869-1970—Juvenile literature. 2. Industrial hygienists—United States—Biography—Juvenile literature. [1. Hamilton, Alice, 1869-1970. 2. Industrial hygienists. 3. Physicians. 4. Social workers.] I. Schulz, Janet, ill. II. Title. III. Series: Creative minds (Minneapolis, Minn.)
RC964.34.H35M36 1992
616.9'803'092—dc20
[B]   91-23634
                                                                           CIP
                                                                            AC

Manufactured in the United States of America

1 2 3 4 5 6 7 8 9 10 01 00 99 98 97 96 95 94 93 92

Table of Contents

Introduction

When Alice Hamilton was born in February 1869, industry in the United States had entered a new period of growth. Ever since the Civil War had ended, the nation had been concentrating its energies on building steamships and extending railroad and telegraph lines. New inventions improved methods of manufacturing chemicals, steel, and machinery. Electricity provided a powerful new energy source. Soon factories were producing more goods and shipping them more easily than ever before.

Other changes were also taking place. As growing factories hired more people, cities grew, too. Industry spread from New England and the East Coast to the rest of the country. Progress was so rapid and exciting that this time of change became known as the Industrial Revolution in both the United States and Europe.

Unfortunately, few Americans thought to wonder

about the possible dangers of these developments. People were too fascinated by the new variety and quantity of goods available to worry about the workers who made them. But Alice Hamilton changed all that.

① Two Kinds of People

Gathering up her skirt with one hand and waving a wooden sword with the other, young Alice Hamilton chased her cousins in and out of the apple orchard. Clash! Bang! went their make-believe weapons as King Arthur and the Knights of the Round Table triumphed over their foes.

No matter how often they acted the scene, the children always had fun. Sometimes they pretended the apple orchard was Sherwood Forest, and they became Robin Hood and his band of merry men. Other times they brought the legend of the Trojan horse to life.

Whatever the children played, there were always plenty of actors to bring the drama to life. The four Hamilton girls—Edith, Alice, Margaret, and Norah—lived only a field away from one set of lively cousins. Other cousins who lived nearby came almost every day to join in the games. Alice and her cousins Agnes and Allen were so close in age and spent so much time together that they were nicknamed "the three A's."

Merrily the three A's and their companions trooped in and out of Alice's house, Agnes's house, and Grandmother Hamilton's house, which were all located on the same property in Fort Wayne, Indiana. Called Old House, Grandmother Hamilton's home was very large and grand. Her husband, a successful businessman and one of the founders of Fort Wayne, had left his family financially secure.

Grandmother Hamilton was a strong supporter of women's rights. Someday, she predicted, women would have the same kinds of jobs as men. Someday they would be given the right to own property and vote. Through her involvement in the women's rights movement, Mrs. Hamilton became a good friend of Susan B. Anthony. The famous suffragist had devoted herself to winning women the right to vote. She had an open invitation to stay at Old House whenever she passed through Indiana.

Like Grandmother Hamilton, Alice's mother was also an independent woman for her time. She encouraged her daughters to speak up about their beliefs. "There are two kinds of people," Gertrude Hamilton declared, "the ones who say, 'Somebody ought to do something about it, but why should it be I?' and those who say, 'Somebody must do something about it, then why not I?'"

"Two kinds of people." Alice never forgot the words. Even as a young girl, she knew which kind of person she wanted to be. She hoped she would do something important, something to help people and to make the world a better place.

But what would that be? This was a hard question for a girl who knew little of the world beyond the Hamilton family. Except for her cousins, Alice did not even know other children in Fort Wayne because Gertrude and Montgomery Hamilton taught their children at home. Alice and her sisters learned Latin from their father, French from their mother, and German from the servants. The girls studied history, religion, and literature, too.

Even Alice's vacations were different from those of less privileged children. Summertime meant going to a vacation spot on Mackinac Island that the Hamilton family had visited every summer since 1879, when Alice was ten years old. The island was located in the straits between Lake Huron and Lake Michigan. Each year as the boat neared the shore, Alice strained to catch glimpses of familiar landmarks. She wanted to make sure nothing had changed in the woods, the pine cliffs, and the pebbled beaches.

Alice enjoyed her carefree childhood, both on Mackinac Island and in Fort Wayne. But as she grew up, some things began to change. She was fourteen when Allen's parents sent him to school in Boston. In Allen's letters to Alice, he included descriptions of his science studies, especially physics. How fascinating it sounded! Eagerly she told her father that she would like to learn physics, too. Mr. Hamilton, a banker and wholesale grocer, had little interest in science himself. "It is all in the encyclopedia," he said. And he was right. The only problem was that Alice could scarcely understand a word of the long, technical account.

A year later, Alice read a book that was much more interesting. It started her thinking about a different branch of science—medicine. *The Merv Oasis* was a detailed travel diary of a diplomat's journey to Persia. Alice imagined herself in the distant land, finding adventure wherever she went. She thought of the people she might meet. Some would be sick, some would be poor. She dreamed of becoming a medical missionary and caring for these people who had no one else to help them.

Alice had many dreams, however, and was not yet ready to study medicine. Two years later, in 1886, her parents sent her to a girls' boarding school in Connecticut, where she studied languages and philosophy. What she learned from her classmates, though, was almost more important than what she learned from her classes. During the required daily walks, Alice had long talks with the other girls. Most of her new friends had attended other schools before this one. They knew more people and had a broader range of experiences than she did. Alice began to realize what an unusual childhood she had led.

By the time Alice returned to Fort Wayne, she had become a determined young woman eager to face the world. She was also eager to see her family, which had grown to include a two-year-old brother, Arthur. By now Alice was old enough to be thinking about marrying and having children of her own. But she was much more interested in a career than in romance. I want to be a doctor, she confided to her sister Edith during one of their many talks about the future.

Like Alice, Edith wanted a career of her own. But Edith was shocked at her sister's unconventional choice. Alice's parents were worried about her decision, too. Many people still considered medicine an unsuitable profession for the "gentle sex," even though forty years had passed since Elizabeth Blackwell had become the first female doctor in the United States. In the years since Dr. Blackwell had made history, about forty-five hundred women had received medical degrees. But female physicians did not have nearly the number of opportunities that men did.

Alice had made her decision carefully, though, and would not be turned from her goal. "As a doctor, I could go anywhere I please," she said, "to far-off lands or city slums—and be quite sure I could be of use anywhere. I should meet all sorts and conditions of men, [and] I should not be tied down to a school or college as a teacher is or have to work under a superior as a nurse must do."

Alice set out to teach herself the sciences she would need to enter medical school. Her dedication and hard work convinced her parents that she had a future as a doctor after all. By 1890 twenty-one-year-old Alice had learned enough on her own and through a small, local school to be accepted at the University of Michigan, one of the top-ranked medical schools in the country. She was one of only thirteen women in her class.

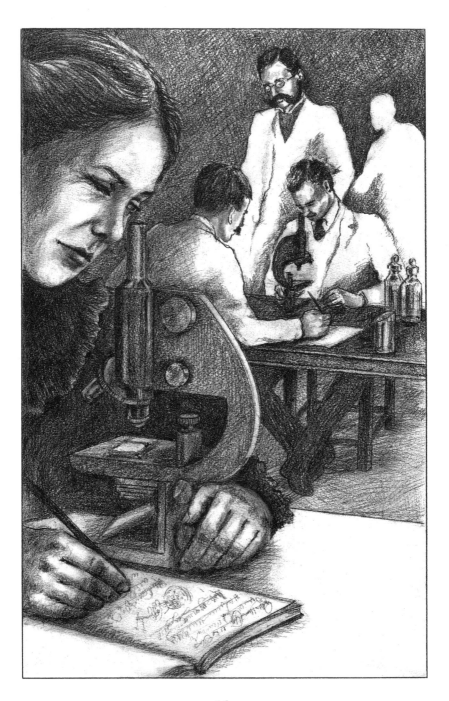

Thirst for Adventure

Peering through a microscope, Alice concentrated on pink- and blue-stained cells. All around her, other young men and women were bent over microscopes, too. There were never quite enough microscopes to go around, so Alice was glad she had arrived at class early enough to claim one. Nothing fascinated her more than viewing the cell, the basic structure of life, through the magnifying lens. In her histology class, she learned to recognize healthy cells, and in pathology class, she examined samples of diseased cells. A hardworking student, she didn't want to miss a thing.

By the time Alice received her medical degree in

1893, she had decided to devote her life to research in pathology. She wanted to study the causes of disease at the most basic level. She knew that when people became sick, some of their cells were affected. What caused these normal cells to change and even die? And how did these changes cause the symptoms of certain illnesses? These were the kinds of questions Alice hoped to answer by examining cells in a laboratory. But first she had to complete an internship. This would give her practical experience with patients and help her find a permanent job once she graduated.

That summer Alice had to leave Mackinac Island early to begin her training. Watching the island grow smaller as her father steered the boat toward the mainland, she felt homesick already. What would her year as an intern be like? she wondered. Would she be able to handle the patients properly?

As soon as she began her duties, Alice was overworked. Her internship was at Northwestern Hospital, a facility for women and children in Minneapolis. She was expected to diagnose illnesses, mix medicines, and deliver babies all by herself. The unscientific methods of the senior doctors did not make her job easier. In a letter to her cousin Agnes, Alice explained her dismay. "All the accurately careful, elaborate work that I have been taught to consider so important is ignored here, and I am expected to make off-hand diagnoses, rapid prescriptions, and meet emergencies without losing my head. None of which I can do at all. There is no laboratory [and] the microscope is not as good as my own."

Alice soon realized she could help patients in spite of these handicaps. But two months later, she was offered another internship in Boston, and she decided to leave Northwestern Hospital. She was lonely in Minneapolis, and the New England Hospital had a fine reputation. Like Northwestern, this was a facility for women and children. (In those days, it was considered improper for female doctors to have men for patients.)

Upon her arrival in Boston, Alice was assigned to the maternity ward. Although she helped deliver many healthy babies, sometimes there was nothing she could do to save an infant or lessen a mother's pain. When one new mother died, Alice could hardly control her grief. The woman had been young and gentle, with much to live for. Alice realized that she was indeed better suited for work in a laboratory than as a practicing doctor. The stress and emotional involvement of patient care was too overwhelming for her.

After several months, Alice was transferred to the dispensary, or home-care clinic. This new position required her to make house calls. Alice never knew where her job would take her—to dingy basements, narrow attics, or tiny rooms over saloons. All over the Boston slums she traveled on foot, sometimes not returning home until after midnight.

On her medical rounds, Alice met many immigrants who could not find work. Often she visited families who were hungry or in need of clothing or coal to heat their homes. Alice put these families in touch with local charities that could help them. In a small but important way, she was beginning to make a difference in the world.

Another intern, named Rachelle Slobodinsky, was also determined to make a difference. Russian by birth, Rachelle had fled her native land at the age of seventeen. When she had arrived in New York, she had taken a job in a sweatshop, a small factory where employees were required to work long hours in hot, dirty rooms. The workers received little pay for their labors. Alice listened to the story of Rachelle's life with fascination and dismay. "Tell me everything," she urged her new friend.

For the first time, Alice felt ashamed of her easy, carefree upbringing. While Alice had been enjoying herself at a private school, Rachelle had been working for a living. "She is only our age, but she has lived through more than we will have when we are sixty," Alice wrote to Agnes.

Alice completed her internship in 1894. She still did not want to be a practicing physician, but she did want to help people who faced hardships like Rachelle's. Somehow she hoped to combine pathology with social work. However, her professors advised her to first study in Germany, which was considered the center for advanced training in pathology. This prospect especially appealed to Alice because her sister Edith, a graduate in literature from Pennsylvania's Bryn Mawr College, was also planning to study in Germany. By 1895 both sisters had returned to Fort Wayne to prepare for the trip.

One day Alice and Edith were busy with their travel plans when their youngest sister, Norah, came bursting into the room. Excitedly, Norah announced that Jane Addams, the famous social worker, was to speak in Fort Wayne that very evening.

Jane Addams! To think that the founder of Hull House would actually be coming through their town! Alice had never seen the poor Chicago neighborhood where Miss Addams had opened her settlement house and offered food, shelter, and other services to those in need. But Alice had read all about the famous social experiment. She knew that Miss Addams and the other resident volunteers at Hull House were always ready to receive their neighbors, usually poor immigrant workers and their families.

That night Alice, Norah, and Agnes attended Jane Addams's speech. Fascinated by everything she heard, Alice realized that she and Miss Addams shared the same goals. Suddenly she knew she had found the perfect way to combine laboratory research and social work. She would become a pathologist, but she would spend her evenings and weekends working in a settlement house.

Shortly after hearing Miss Addams speak, Alice left with Edith for Germany, where they studied first in Leipzig and later in Munich. Although she enjoyed making German friends, Alice did not learn much pathology that she had not already known. In class women were officially "invisible." In order to attend one special lecture,

Alice had to be escorted by an elderly physician to a chair in the corner of the room before the other doctors entered. And wherever she went, the same question seemed to follow her: "If American women go into science, who will darn the stockings?"

When she returned to the United States, Alice could not find a job, so she continued her study of pathology at Johns Hopkins University, in Baltimore. A year later, in 1897, she accepted a position as a professor at the Women's Medical College of Northwestern University, in Chicago. Right away Alice knew where she wanted to live!

Nervous but hopeful, Alice went to Hull House to speak with Miss Addams. Just as Alice had imagined, Miss Addams was sympathetic and kind. But she did not have good news. All the rooms at Hull House were occupied by other volunteers. There was no room for another resident.

Alice did not pause to rest. She marched several miles north to another settlement house called the Commons. Once more she was turned away. Tired and disappointed, Alice wondered how she would achieve her goal of combining science and social work.

That summer Alice turned to the quiet beauty

of Mackinac Island for comfort. She knew that medical work alone could not satisfy her thirst for adventure. Never had she felt so uncertain about her future. Then one morning the mail boat brought her a letter from Jane Addams. Alice was thrilled to learn that a room at Hull House would be available after all. The young doctor could begin her life at the settlement house that October.

Medical Mystery

In many ways, Hull House, with its elegant design and high ceilings, reminded Alice of Old House. But her life in the lovely old settlement house was nothing like her sheltered childhood. Although Alice had seen poverty in Boston, in Chicago she lived in the middle of it.

The men and women who visited Hull House worked long hours in factories for very little money. Their homes were small, stuffy rooms in crowded tenement apartments. Rats scampered through the alleys around these buildings, and smelly garbage overflowed its containers.

Because her patients were also her neighbors, she developed an even stronger understanding of their hopes and hardships than she had developed with her patients in Boston.

Anxious to help everyone, Alice made house calls to sick children and founded a well-baby clinic where mothers could bring their young children for checkups and baths. She tried to teach people how to prevent illnesses, though often this was difficult. The women did not understand how bacteria spread, and at thirty years old, Alice looked too young to be an expert. But her gentle smile and friendly concern appealed to parents as well as their children.

Besides caring for her neighbors' health, Alice wanted to enrich their lives with beauty and learning. Enthusiastically she taught art and English classes at night. She also helped with the boys' club and supervised the men's athletic club. On weekends she liked to take children for picnics in the country. The grateful youngsters often followed her noisily as she bustled down the streets near Hull House. How she longed to help these boys and girls find a better life!

Sometimes Alice picketed with the children's parents when they went on strike for higher wages and shorter working hours. Risking arrest, she held her sign high and marched back and forth in front of the factories.

When Alice had been at Hull House five years, the women's medical school where she taught became part of the men's school. The new coeducational school did not have a position for Alice. So she found a new job as a bacteriologist at the Memorial Institute for Infectious Diseases. But Alice's life at Hull House was more absorbing than her life in the laboratory.

The more Alice got to know the factory workers at Hull House, the more they told her about their illnesses and physical disabilities. An alarming pattern began to emerge as Alice listened to the tales of her neighbors. Pale, thin, and prematurely wrinkled, the painters and lead-factory workers suffered from indigestion and sometimes had trouble moving their wrists and hands properly—all symptoms of lead poisoning. Workers in steel mills told of breathing carbon monoxide, while those employed in the stockyards seemed to have high rates of pneumonia and rheumatism.

Some people claimed fatigue was responsible for these problems, but Alice suspected that poor conditions in the factories were ruining the workers' health.

In 1907 Alice discovered a book by Thomas Oliver that confirmed her suspicions. It was called *Dangerous Trades*, and it was all about the health risks of certain jobs. Thomas Oliver had done a fine job of surveying the British industrial scene. After finishing the volume, Alice decided to see what had been written about American factories.

To her amazement, Alice could not find any literature on the subject. She turned to other doctors for help, and here, too, she was in for a surprise. American workers did not suffer from industrial poisons, her colleagues declared.

Alice had lived too long at Hull House to accept these easy answers. All around her, Americans were suffering dreadful disabilities and sometimes *dying*—simply from doing their jobs!

Something had to be done, she realized. Someone had to prove what was happening in American factories. Although laws had been passed in several states in an attempt to protect workers' health, little had been achieved. Alice felt she was striking out in a brand-new field.

Alice continued to talk to workers. She investigated every clue about their mysterious illnesses. In September 1908, she published her first article on the subject, encouraging Americans to rally for better working conditions. She also addressed the issue of women's health. Women who worked with lead suffered even more severe disorders than men who worked with lead, she believed. Women often worked in warm, damp surroundings such as laundries or canning factories. These conditions increased the risk of heart disease and tuberculosis and caused some pregnant women to lose their babies. Soon many people knew of Alice's interest, but few people were able to supply her with proof of her theories.

Finally, when Alice was thirty-nine years old, a visitor named John Andrews came to Hull House with important evidence to show her. He had done a study of a strange illness called phossy jaw. The terrible disease caused facial bones to slip out of place and the jaw to swell up painfully. In severe cases, patients lost an eye or a jawbone. Only one group of people ran the risk of phossy jaw—workers in match factories. Their illness had been linked to the phosphorus they breathed while performing their jobs.

Eagerly Alice pored over the report. She knew all about phossy jaw, but other medical experts claimed the disease was unknown in the United States. Here was proof they were wrong. John Andrews had discovered more than 150 cases of phossy jaw among American match workers! Alice could use this information to educate others and to stir up interest within the medical community.

Within two years of the report's publication, a new law banned the use of phosphorus in match making. Rapidly, a new substance called sesqui-sulphide was substituted for phosphorus. Soon phossy jaw was a disease of the past.

The work of Alice Hamilton, John Andrews, and other observant people was slowly bringing change to American industry. In December 1908, the governor of Illinois created an Occupational Disease Committee. Already considered an expert in the field, Alice was asked to join the nine-member panel. And since Alice knew more about industrial medicine than anyone else on the committee, she was asked to be the managing director of the survey. Together the experts would study industrial hygiene, or cleanliness, in Illinois factories and make a list of dangerous jobs.

Alice felt challenged and determined. But she

was overwhelmed at the same time. No one knew all the occupational hazards facing the workers of Illinois. Alice could only hope to discover them as she went along.

Taking time away from the laboratory, Alice got right to work. Her special topic in the survey was lead poisoning, a much bigger field than she had first imagined. Touring factories all around the state, she interviewed workers in trades known to expose their workers to lead.

What is the hardest part of your job?

How long have you worked here?

Are you as healthy now as you were when you began this job?

These were the kinds of questions Alice asked the surprised workers. No one had ever taken an interest in their lives like this. Some men were afraid of losing their jobs if they spoke with Alice. Others, responding to her warmth and concern, told her what she needed to know about their jobs and their health.

But Alice wanted a broader picture than her factory visits could give her. She spent hours reading patient histories in hospitals all over the state. When she discovered cases of lead poisoning, she went to see the victims in their homes.

She spoke with their families. Many of them were immigrants, alone and bewildered in this new country. Alice let them know that she cared what happened to them.

On one visit, Alice was puzzled by a man with severe stomach pain and trembling hands. From his hospital records, she was certain the man had lead poisoning. But she did not know why. He told Alice that he put enamel on bathtubs— not a job she associated with high exposure to lead. So Alice set out to investigate. She found workers sprinkling ground enamel over tubs that were hot enough to melt the fine, white powder. The air was heavy with enamel dust. The workers could not help but breathe it in.

When Alice explained what she was doing, one of them gave her a sample of the powder to take home. Her detective work paid off. She tested the powder in the laboratory and was shocked to learn the enamel was twenty percent lead. Even the more advanced Europeans had failed to note this. No longer was the man's illness a mystery. Grimly Alice added enameling to her list of dangerous trades.

No one involved in the survey expected Alice to do anything about the conditions she found—

except to report them. But how many people would suffer health problems before changes were made? Someone had to speak for them now. Alice still remembered her mother's long-ago words. "Two kinds of people," Gertrude Hamilton had said. Alice realized that reporting what she had seen was not enough.

Although it was not part of her job, Alice tried to convince employers to improve working conditions. One day she spoke with Edward Cornish, vice president of the National Lead Works, a company that owned several factories in Chicago. Bravely she told him his men were being poisoned.

At first Mr. Cornish was angry at her accusations. But Alice was so kind and sincere in spite of her charges that he stopped to think. "I don't believe you are right," he said at last, "but I can see you do." And he told Alice that if she could show that his workers were being poisoned, he would do everything she asked.

Rising to the challenge, Alice proved her detective skills by discovering twenty-two cases of lead poisoning among his workers. Mr. Cornish was surprised and impressed. He kept his promise to Alice and reformed his factories.

Blazing the Trail
in Industrial Medicine

Like a real detective, Alice followed every clue as she worked to establish the relationships between workers' illnesses and their jobs. "This industrial diseases work is like trying to make one's way through a jungle and not even being able to find an opening," she wrote in 1910. But Alice made her own openings. Before the committee submitted its report in January 1911, Alice had discovered seventy-seven lead-related trades and documented more than five hundred cases of lead poisoning.

Responding to the hard evidence the committee had uncovered, the Illinois legislature passed an occupational disease law in 1911. Now employers were required to follow safety precautions and provide monthly checkups for workers who handled certain dangerous substances. Six other states also passed occupational-disease laws that year. This was tremendous progress, but Alice knew there was much more to do. If only the American medical profession would take a greater interest in industry, her job would be much easier.

The members of the committee knew this, too. They decided to send Alice to the International Congress on Occupational Accidents and Diseases in Brussels, Belgium, to learn about advances in the field. Although this was a wonderful opportunity, it meant Alice had even less time for her laboratory work. But she believed she could make greater contributions to the new field of industrial medicine than to pathology. Eagerly she set off for the conference.

In Brussels Alice heard noted European experts speak on all aspects of industrial medicine. Alice spoke, too. She presented a paper about white lead, a substance containing lead that was used in some paints. The European doctors were very interested in her comments. What is the rate of lead poisoning in different jobs? they asked her. What are your laws for regulating the dangerous trades?

To Alice's disgrace, she had no answers to their questions. Finally a Belgian doctor ended the discussion, saying, "It is well known that there is no industrial hygiene in the United States."

Alice felt her face grow hot with embarrassment.

Charles O'Neill was also embarrassed. He was the U.S. Commissioner of Labor and one of the few other Americans at the conference. Shortly after Alice returned to the United States, Mr. O'Neill sent her a letter asking for a very big commitment. Would Alice do for the entire nation what she was doing for Illinois?

At forty-two years old, Alice had reached a crossroads in her life. If she accepted the new position, she did not know when she would get back to laboratory work. She also knew that as a federal investigator, she would have many responsibilities and few privileges. On her own, she would have to identify and locate factories. She would have to convince the owners to let her inside and make her own guidelines for how to proceed. And she would not get paid until each report was finished.

These seemed like hard terms, but industrial medicine meant too much to Alice for her to pass up such an exciting opportunity. She accepted the position in Washington, D.C., and never returned to research again. She did, however, continue to spend time at Hull House. Although Alice's new job took her all over the East and

Midwest, she still considered the settlement her home and spent as much time there as possible. It was always good to return to friends who understood her commitment and enthusiasm.

For her first national survey, Alice again chose lead and set about locating and visiting factories. Some foremen in these factories must have bristled at the thought of allowing a stranger to come in and criticize their management—and it must not have helped that she was a woman. But Alice would explain that she was there to help them, not to stir up resentment with the workers. Happy, healthy employees made for a better-running factory, she would point out. Alice's quiet sincerity and unfailing courtesy convinced the owners that she was their friend. Factory after factory opened its doors for her inspection.

And factory after factory failed to meet the most basic health standards. Everywhere she went, Alice found men eating their lunches with lead-encrusted hands, men whose hair was plastered with lead. Worst of all, she found men breathing in the dangerous lead dust and fumes.

Sometimes the conditions she found made her angry, but she stayed calm. In spite of everything she saw, Alice believed that factory owners cared about their employees just as Mr. Cornish did. So after she inspected a factory, she would convince the owners and managers to make important changes. She told them how to use fans and vents to pull fresh air into the workrooms and minimize the dust. She encouraged them to provide regular medical checkups for all employees.

Although men still dominated the medical profession, Alice felt that being a woman helped her achieve reforms in industrial hygiene. "Employers and doctors both appeared more willing to listen to me as I told them their duties than they would have been if I had been a man," she wrote years later. "It seemed natural and right that a woman should put care of the producing workman ahead of the value of the thing he was producing."

After five years of studying lead, Alice began to investigate the rubber industry. But other issues were claiming her attention, too. Europe was fighting the Great War, World War I. Alice, who labored ceaselessly for the lives of people on the job, was horrified at the thought of young men losing their lives on the battlefield.

Jane Addams shared Alice's desire for a peaceful Europe. In 1915 the famous social worker decided to attend the International Congress of

Women to protest the war. Alice made plans to travel to the Netherlands with her.

Alice Hamilton and Jane Addams arrived at The Hague, Netherlands, just as the first session was about to open. Twelve warring and neutral nations were represented at the eleven-hundred-person congress. Most of the women, including the Americans, were not allowed to vote in their own countries. They may have had no part in declaring the war, but they would do anything they could to stop it.

When Jane Addams was asked to visit government leaders in France, Germany, Austria-Hungary, Italy, Holland, and Switzerland, Alice went along as her unofficial companion. Disappointed but not really surprised when these personal appeals failed to end the war, Alice returned to the United States. There was nothing she could do to protect the soldiers, but there was another group of people she might be able to help. More determined than ever, she turned her attention to workers in the rapidly growing munitions, or weapons, industry.

Dangers Above
and Below

Pursued by a cloud of foul-smelling, red smoke, Alice fled across the field. She felt choked by the fumes, and she gasped for breath. But she did manage to outrun the dangerous smoke from the picric acid factory. The hazardous chemical was used to make ammunition.

Alice found herself among the withered stalks of a cornfield. The men who had once farmed the land now worked in the factory making wartime chemicals. Although the United States had not yet entered World War I, Americans were helping to supply France with the explosives it needed. Factory accidents like this one had killed the remaining plants in the abandoned fields.

All around her, Alice saw workers who had hurried from the factory when the poisonous fumes had begun to fill the building. Most of them had been stained yellow from daily exposure to the picric acid. Because of their coloring, the workers were called "canaries" by the townspeople.

Alice had seen her first canaries only a few hours earlier at a New Jersey railroad station. As she watched the terrible cloud dissolve in the sky, she remembered the man she had met at the station. This canary was a black man with bright orange nails, hair, and eyebrows. A yellow pallor covered his cheeks. The palms of his hands were dyed a vivid yellow. "Is the factory dangerous?" Alice had asked.

"Not the yellow stuff ain't," he replied, "but there's a red smoke comes off when the yellow stuff is making, and it like to knocks you out, and if you don't run, it gets you. You don't suspicion nothing much, you goes home and eats your supper and goes to bed, and then in the night you starts to choke up, and by morning you're dead."

Alice found the same bleak conditions in other factories. At a smokeless-powder factory in Virginia, she watched explosive particles being poured from a large pipe into a bin. They looked harmless, but her guide explained that sometimes sparks were produced when the particles rubbed together. If that happened, he warned, she should run for the nearest window. Alice stared. Jump out of a third-floor window? Then she saw the long safety chute leading to the ground. Fortunately she didn't have to use it.

Alice wanted to study army and navy arsenals as well as privately owned factories. The army welcomed her inspections of its manufacturing and storage sites, but the navy refused to grant her permission.

Finally Alice arranged an interview with the assistant secretary of the navy in Washington. The young man listened to Alice very carefully, then called a high-ranking admiral into the meeting. Soon Alice received the permission she needed. Thanking the assistant secretary for his speed and efficiency, Alice never dreamed that the man, Franklin Roosevelt, would one day be president of the United States.

After the United States entered the war in April 1917, Alice's work became even more demanding. Almost overnight, explosives manufacturers were required to increase production. But Alice soon noticed a more important change that could not be measured in numbers. The munitions workers' health was suddenly a matter of national concern.

Factories needed their employees to stay healthy in order to produce more weapons. As a result, doctors began to take a real interest in workers' welfare. Lawmakers and doctors began to talk about Alice's work and the solutions she was suggesting.

After the war, the interest in munitions workers' health spread to other industries. Industrial medicine was recognized as a respected branch of science, and Alice Hamilton was often credited as its pioneer. There were still hazardous jobs left to explore, and new ones were created as technology continued to develop. But Alice's work would never be quite so difficult again.

Reflecting the new interest in workers' health, the Harvard University Medical School established a department of industrial hygiene. Doctors had to be trained to meet the challenges of this new field. But who would teach them? The dean of the school hoped that Alice Hamilton would. He offered her a position as assistant professor. If she accepted the job, she would be the first female faculty member at the famous university.

But Alice liked working for the Labor Department and was not interested in studying department stores, as the dean had suggested.

Postponing her decision, she turned her thoughts to her upcoming investigation of Arizona copper mines.

On a chilly January morning in 1919, Alice set off from Hull House for one of the best adventures of her career. She was almost fifty years old. She looked and dressed like a young grandmother. But soon Alice found herself doing things few grandmothers would care to imitate.

In the Globe-Miami mining district of Arizona, she traded her long skirt for overalls and a helmet with a built-in lamp. Bravely she stepped into a "cage," which must have seemed a strange name for an elevator without walls. Alice had nothing to cling to as the cage lowered her shakily into the depths of the Old Dominion Mine. Eight hundred feet below the surface of the earth, the elevator came to rest.

Now Alice's adventure really began. Following her guide, she climbed up a slope on her hands and knees to watch the miners operate their jackhammers. With these heavy machines, they drilled into the tunnel walls in search of copper. Some miners had reported that the powerful vibrations of the jackhammers were ruining their health. After a day in the mines, they felt sick and weak.

Alice watched them carefully, noting that some of the jackhammers had water attachments to dampen the rocks. Miners could then drill without raising as much dust. But the men had not complained to Alice about the dust. It was the vibrations of the jackhammers that they believed were making them sick.

Alice explored the entire mine. She climbed down an eighty-foot ladder into one pit. She crawled across another pit on a high railing. The rungs on the railing were so far apart that Alice had to stretch to reach them. One false move and she was sure she would fall into the blackness below. Forcing herself to remain calm, she slowly and carefully followed her guide.

When Alice emerged into the daylight, she was certain that dust posed a greater threat to the miners' health than the jackhammers. At other mines and at meetings with workers and doctors, she urged more widespread use of the wet drill. She told them that she had tried the jackhammer and found it extremely uncomfortable, but she did not know if the vibrations alone could cause permanent injury.

A study of department-store workers could never compare with her experience in Arizona. And yet as she headed home, Alice felt disappointed. She would have liked to teach at Harvard. It would have given her great satisfaction to train new doctors in industrial medicine.

To Alice's delight, she found a letter from Harvard awaiting her at Hull House. The university was offering her a half-time teaching appointment. This would leave her six months each year to work for the Labor Department. And she would not be required to do the department-store study. Gratefully Alice sat down to write her acceptance.

6

Lasting Contributions

Alice Hamilton and Jane Addams were crossing the ocean again. It was April 1919, the spring before Alice was to begin her duties at Harvard. The two women were on their way to the second International Congress for Women, in Zurich, Switzerland, to discuss the effects of the war.

When they arrived at the meeting, they heard shocking stories of children starving all over Germany. Until the defeated countries agreed to all the peace terms, the winning countries were preventing the delivery of food to Germany. Alice was saddened and angered by this food blockade. After the congress was over, she and Jane Addams toured the hungry nation for the American Friends Service Committee, a Quaker organization dedicated to providing food for the needy.

The children Alice met were pale and weak. At

a care center near Frankfurt, she saw school-children eating lunch. They were so thin she could count their ribs, but all they had to eat was soup made mostly of water with a few grains and chopped leaves in it. Alice resolved to take the problem home to the people of the United States. If only she could make her fellow citizens see the children through her eyes, she was certain they would be willing to help.

Back in Boston, Alice began teaching classes at Harvard. In her free time, she made speeches asking people to donate money to Quaker relief centers in Germany. But not everyone viewed the problem as she did. Many people still thought of the Germans as enemies. How could good Americans want to help their enemies? they asked.

Finally one university official asked Alice to stop her activities. People will not contribute to the school while there is a pro-German on the faculty, he explained. But who else would speak for the hungry German children? Alice kept right on asking for money.

She also kept right on visiting factories. When her official connection to the Labor Department ended in 1920, she continued her investigations with her Harvard colleagues. One important study involved the manufacture of felt hats, an industry in which large numbers of workers acted so strangely that they were called "mad hatters." Lewis Carroll had used the phrase humorously in his book *Alice in Wonderland*. But this real-life Alice knew there was nothing funny about the trembling limbs and irritable behavior of the sick men, exposed to deadly mercury nitrate every day. With her university associates, Alice worked to increase public awareness of this health menace. Gradually laws limited the use of mercury, and the felt-hat industry was pressured into replacing mercury nitrate with a nontoxic substance.

Alice's studies of mercury poisoning in the felt-hat industry and quicksilver mines, as well as her earlier government studies of industries in which carbon monoxide and aniline dye were used, helped pave the way for workers' compensation laws in several states. Under these regulations, men and women who were injured or became ill as a result of their jobs were entitled to financial support from their employers. Because manufacturers and insurance companies did not want to pay this extra money, they worked harder for safe, healthy factories.

Classes, field work, and other commitments

kept Alice almost constantly on the go. Between 1924 and 1930, she served as a member of the League of Nations Health Committee. After her first league meeting in Geneva, Switzerland, she toured the Soviet Union for a firsthand look at its industrial hygiene. And in 1925, she published a highly praised six-hundred-page textbook on industrial medicine.

After her retirement from Harvard in 1935, Alice went to live with her sister Margaret and a friend in Hadlyme, Connecticut. At sixty-six years old, Alice was energetic and keenly aware of what still needed to be done. She renewed her association with the Department of Labor and studied the viscose rayon, or artificial silk, industry. Based on her work, the Pennsylvania legislature passed its first workers' compensation law.

When she wasn't traveling, Alice enjoyed the community life at Hadlyme and took an active interest in the small town's affairs. She liked to garden and to chat with friends. She did not feel like an important or famous person at all.

One day Eleanor Roosevelt spoke at Connecticut College, near Hadlyme. Alice still treasured her memory of Franklin Roosevelt as the assistant secretary who had helped her during World War I.

set up at the Harvard School of Public Health. Two years later, a dormitory at Connecticut College was named after Alice and her sister Edith, who had become a famous writer.

But perhaps one of Alice's least expected and most moving compliments came just seven years after her retirement. As she and a guest entered the Department of Labor's private dining room in Washington, everyone in the room stood up in silent tribute. Afterward the government officials stopped by her table to greet her personally.

Even in retirement, Alice was guided by her mother's advice. Whenever there was something that needed to be done, Alice was ready to do it. One of her last public stands was to sign a protest against American involvement in Vietnam. Alice was ninety-four years old. As long as she lived, her determination to create a better world would never waver.

Afterword

On February 27, 1969, Alice Hamilton, propped up in bed and wearing a pink nightgown, greeted a six-person delegation from the Women's International League for Peace and Freedom. It was her one-hundredth birthday, and people from all over the country were calling her and sending flowers and cards. Even President Nixon sent a telegram thanking Alice for her "lasting contributions to the well-being of our people and of men and women everywhere." Some friends baked a birthday cake for her. It had six roses and one bright candle.

Alice's mind wandered a good deal during her last years. Sometimes it was difficult to know what she was thinking. As she celebrated her birthday, she might have been remembering the children at Hull House, her peace missions to Europe, or any of her countless visits to dangerous factories.

The workers she had met in those factories were old now, too. Some would have grandchildren or even great-grandchildren old enough to have jobs. Wherever they worked, the new generations benefited from Alice's studies. She had helped create a new atmosphere in which industry and medical science cooperated to protect workers.

Alice Hamilton died in September 1970. That December a federal law was passed that gave the government the right to enforce health standards in privately owned businesses. Thanks to Alice's dedication and hard work, men and women in all sorts of jobs could look forward to the same kind of healthy, active old age that she herself had enjoyed.

Select Bibliography

Books

Grant, Madeleine P. *Alice Hamilton: Pioneer Doctor in Industrial Medicine*. New York: Abelard-Schuman, 1967.

Hamilton, Alice. *Exploring the Dangerous Trades: The Autobiography of Alice Hamilton*. Boston: Little, Brown, and Company, 1943.

Sicherman, Barbara. *Alice Hamilton: A Life in Letters*. Cambridge: Harvard University Press, 1984.

Articles

Felton, Jean Spencer, M.D. "Industrial Health as a Specialty: A Medical Field of Interest to Women's Physicians," *Journal of the American Medical Women's Association* (June 1947): 294-299.

Hamilton, Alice. "Pioneering in Industrial Medicine," *Journal of the American Medical Women's Association* (June 1947): 292-293.

Hamilton, Alice. "A Woman of Ninety Looks at Her World," *The Atlantic* (September 1961): 51-55.

——. "Edith and Alice Hamilton: Students in Germany," *The Atlantic* (March 1965): 129-132.

——. "Nineteen Years in the Poisonous Trades," *Harper's* (October 1929): 580-591.

Hardy, Harriet L., ed. *Journal of Occupational Medicine* (February 1972). Special issue dedicated to Alice Hamilton.

Sergeant, Elizabeth Shepley. "Alice Hamilton, M.D.: Crusader for Health in Industry," *Harper's* (May 1926): 763-770.

Urbano, Judy. "Doctor's Life Spanned Hull House, Labor Strife" and "Pioneering Doctor Made Hadlyme Her Last Home." Parts I, II. *The Gazette*, October 26 and November 2, 1978. (Courtesy of the Lyme Public Library, Lyme, Connecticut.)

——. "Dr. Alice Hamilton Celebrates 100th Birthday: Famed Industrial Toxicologist is Honored for her Work in Mines and Factories," Special to *The New York Times*, February 29, 1969.

Other sources include various newspaper and journal articles, biographical dictionaries, a biography of Edith Hamilton, and two doctoral dissertations.